How to save money for Dummies

Oscar Brown

Contents

Introduction

In this book we will learn 5 savings methods that really work so you can save a lot of money save a lot of money without needing to earn more.

Hello, my name is Oscar Brown, and my mission through this book is to help you achieve personal and financial success financial success by becoming the best version of yourself. version of yourself.

So, pay attention and you will learn that you are just saving your money the wrong way.

Situation of a normal person

The truth is, it's no surprise that the vast majority of people don't have enough money saved to get by for more than a month without receiving income from a job, a business or being supported by someone else on whom they depend.

In fact, according to studies, 60% of American adults do not even have $1,000 saved. According to these studies, during the different crises that different countries have gone through, people start to save more (the proportion of savings increases according to the income of different households).

but when the country's economy is doing relatively well, even though some continue to complain, this proportion of savings decreases. What this shows us is that we are truly capable of saving but we do not do it unless we have a real motivation, or failing that, as it is really possible, through a better financial education.

It is important to clarify that this is independent, absolutely independent of the income level of each person, no matter if you earn $100 a year, $1000 a year or $10 million a year, saving is a habit. It is a way of managing your money, it is a mentality, it is really a capacity that we have, that if we develop it from the beginning, it can permeate and grow with us to the levels that we ourselves grow.

But in the same way, there are people that when they earn 1000 dollars a month they spend it all, when they earn 5000 dollars a month they spend it all, and when they earn 10 thousand dollars a month they spend it all, and at all times they live as if they do not have enough money.

It's not that it's not enough money, it's that he doesn't know how to manage it. However, it is not always easy to save money and simply manage the income you receive very well, distribute it and make it work.

So let's start by looking at 5 tricks that have worked for me AND have worked for people I know. Let's take a look at the first one.

Purchases Needed?

We start with reducing impulse purchases. The truth is that if we ask practically anyone, ¿are you a compulsive shopper? they are going to say no, they are not a compulsive shopper.

But if we take and analyze the income and expenses of all those people, the categories, the products they bought, the services they acquired, we could very likely find 3 elements; 3 items that were not necessary or that they could have postponed, that they simply made the decision to acquire them in haste. This is what we mean when we talk about impulse buying.

The most important thing is to learn to identify the desire to buy right now. In other words, when you are faced with a purchase decision (which hopefully you will postpone), it is simply the moment to move from thinking about whether you want to buy it or not (from analyzing the benefits for your life or imagining or visualizing yourself having that product), to the moment when you take out your money, your card (your debit or credit card) and pay, and the more distance and time there is between those two moments, the better.

Why, because they put you in control. Probably if you postpone for tomorrow a purchase that today you thought to do immediately at the supermarket because you saw something that was on discount (in theory you were going to save, but in reality you were going to spend), or something like that; the next day you say: "well, on second thought, I don't need that, on second thought, I will see where else I can get a better price" (which we will talk about later in this book).

If several days later you are still the same, with the intention or the desire to buy, you consider that it is really necessary, you can definitely do it, you will know yourself consciously if it is really worth doing it, but with this you free yourself from the need to feel like that shot of dopamine that occurs at the moment in which you decide to buy immediately.

The power to throw away change

The name of the chapter sounds a little harsh, but let me explain what I mean by this second trick. The second savings method that really works is to round up the change. Personally I've been keeping detailed track of all my income and expenses for many, many years, so every time I buy something, I simply write it down in an app that I carry on my phone and watch, so I'm in control at all times.

Not to advertise or anything, personally I recommend the app "money maker" After entering everything we buy a day in different categories (we will talk about this later) we will have a little more accurate control of how much we spend, because we know that even if you think you know what you spend it on, at the end of the day you never have the money you expect; is that when I bought something; at that time I used more cash than today, if I bought something, for example, in dollars we are talking about $10. 5 dollars I would write it down as if it were $11 dollars, the coins or the change I would just keep it and I still put it in little jars.

Putting it in little jars and at the end of the month I would go to the bank and deposit it. Every month I was really surprised at the amount of money that could go into that change, that when I didn't pay attention to it, it would just happen that sometimes I would buy a candy or do this or do that, or simply when I didn't keep that money, I had nothing left at the end of the month.

If you do this and adapt to the fact that things simply cost a little bit more, from one moment to the next you are automatically setting aside more money than it would seem possible and at the end of the month you will have a reserve.

For people who use practically only electronic money like me, you can also do it by transferring to a savings fund, a trust account, investment fund or another separate savings account, or whatever, the changes (the differences in the different purchases that you have). That can be done just like with coins, it can be done with electronic money, there is no excuse, the question is to make it a habit.

Small steps

Method number 3, is to commit yourself to save a fixed rate, a fixed and strict percentage of all your income. You just received 100 dollars and let's say the savings is 10%, you have to set aside 10 dollars, put it in a place or in an account where you know you are not going to take it out (there are different financial products that can help you in this regard, but the best financial product is your financial education), so that you know that you are not going to spend that money for anything in the world, it's that simple.

If you commit yourself to a specific rate, to a percentage, to a proportion, it doesn't matter if you earn 100 dollars, 10 dollars, 1000 dollars, 100 thousand dollars, you are always going to be strict with your percentage. Some people even distribute their income in different categories, whether it is for savings, investments, fixed expenses, luxuries, likes, etc.

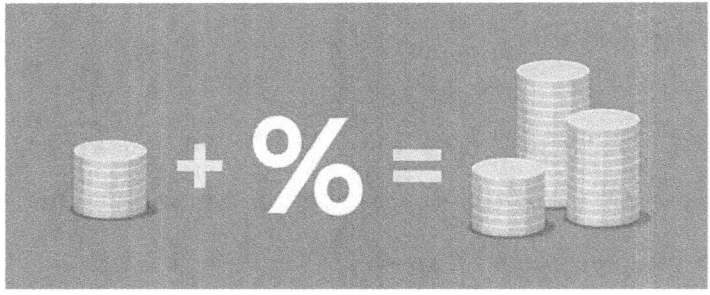

That's also possible to do, but let's start with the basics. Let's say you are currently having difficulties with saving (if you look at your savings and you don't have much money or if the only savings you have made in your life, you have spent on a vacation or the last phone or anything else and you are not really saving thinking ahead), it is important that you implement this technique with all the money that comes into your life, regardless of the amount, I repeat: with a proportion.

Start with something relatively low, maybe 5%, maybe less than that would be too little or 10%, you will see how much. Try to be as strict as possible and do everything possible to survive with the rest. It doesn't matter if you have debts, if you have expenses, if you have obligations, set that percentage aside as a savings.

This is a fundamental skill for your success that in several months or years, will have you in a much better financial situation than the one you are in today, but only if you start doing it now.

Expense control

Number 4, my favorite: analyze all your expenses, at least for a month (30 days), and practically start to write down each of the movements, to write down the categories of expenses, some banks allow you to do that automatically or you can purchase an application for your phone, there are just tons that allow you to do it.

This is where the application that I mentioned before comes in, it will allow you to keep the expenses in several categories, and it will make a graph where you will see what you spent and you can also enter your income to have the balance.

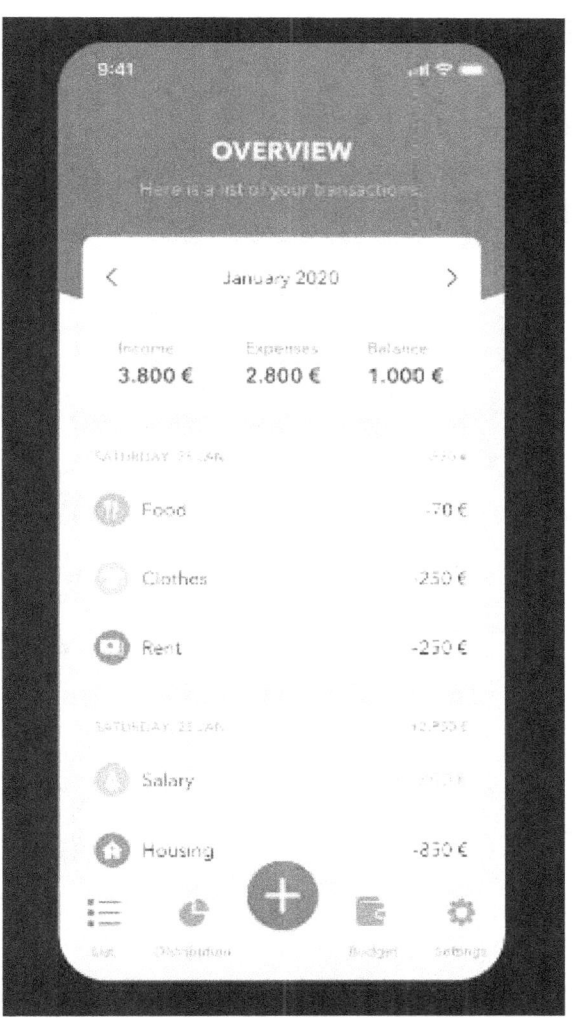

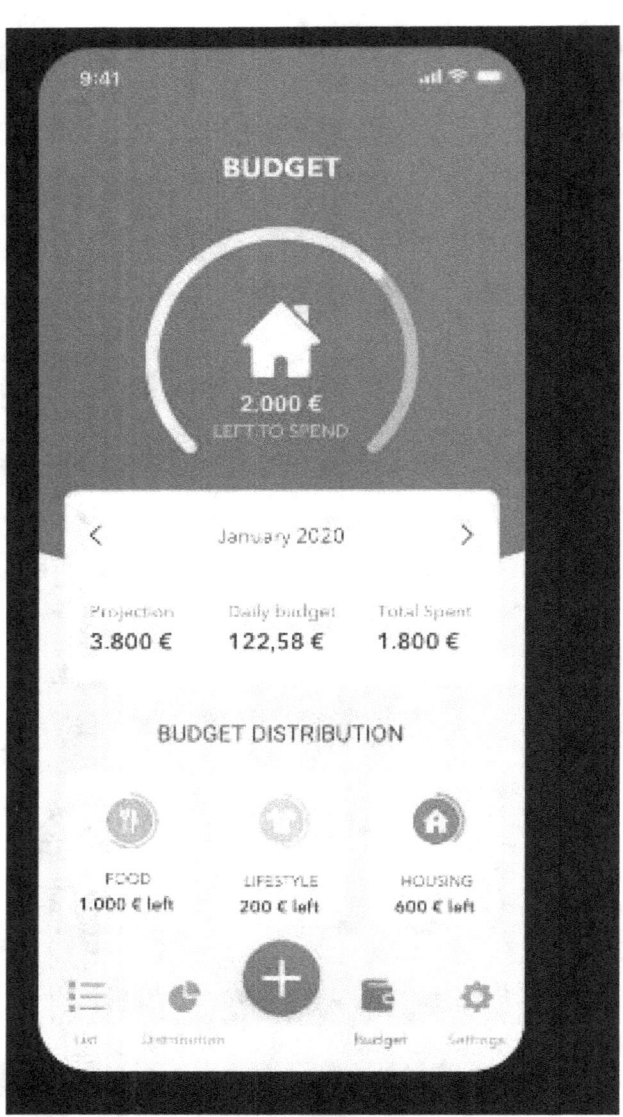

The case is that you have exactly distributed all your movements, here we are not going to exclude anything, we are not going to leave aside this one because it is very economic, this one because..., no! "we only write down the most important".

Everything, we are going to write down absolutely all your movements, and then we take that data and say what are my obligatory expenses, my basic expenses, the minimum I need.

For example, I cannot not buy food, logically it is not something negotiable, I cannot not pay the electricity or water service in my house, in short. But then, after that we say: Okay, is there any way to optimize the obligatory? Sometmes there are ways to save, for example, buying n different places the same product, through different strategies such as buying in quantity.

Maybe in the mandatory items there is not much to optimize, but then we analyze which are the other categories of expenses, unnecessary expenses, luxuries, eating out, impulse purchases, etc.

For these categories we are going to define a limit, a limit that when you have already reached that limit, let's suppose that you say: Okay, my income is 1000 dollars, my mandatory expenses are 600, I am going to define a maximum limit of 200 for luxuries, tastes, etc. And you reached 200 and today it is only 5 and you have the whole month left, so the rest of the month you can't spend a penny on those things.

So you also learn to acquire self-control, you learn to understand how to manage your money, to perceive how to spend it and practically to know in advance if that is a good decision or not financially.

And finally, as you earn more money, clearly many of those things will improve because it's not about limiting yourself, it's about controlling your money to the maximum, and optimizing it to be able to grow. So that when you have more income, you have a better command of all that income.

Do I get promotions or buy more?

Method number 5: is to take advantage of discounts and promotions, but be careful, it is not about going crazy. There are people who spend more gasoline, I knew the case of an economics professor who went to another city in his car, to save a few pesos in the market and return (in the end, he did save some money, we are talking about 10, 20 dollars per market, a market that could cost 200 or 300 dollars and still with gasoline maybe it was a little cheaper), but how much time was he spending? That is also important.

There are many people who do not put a price on their time and that can be calculated. But then, yes, there are situations where I could be a little bit smarter about the purchases I make. I easily go to the supermarket all year round and I can see that there are seasons in which some products are on sale, they are on discount.

Then I can practically match the date of my purchase of those products with the date they go on discount or I can buy in advance, either personal hygiene products or other non-perishable products that can last for a long time, when they are on 2 for 1 (on sale): or this or that, in quantity, and thus save a lot of money not only in the short term but in the medium term.

And if you are smart and have good self-control, you can even use credit cards. Even the credit cards of some specific brands or malls or supermarkets, which give you special discounts on some products, or in the whole store.

Use them, pay them at an installment, pay them without interest, even if those cards had handling fees, annuities or maintenance, maybe you could have a positive difference that benefits you.

The key is not to pay interest, the key is not to buy these kinds of things in installments or on credit because maybe you are going to lose absolutely everything to maximize how this leverage, in any case it is about looking for opportunities in which you can reduce your expenses intelligently). And, watch out! You have to know that when we see an opportunity to save money by paying, we are not really saving money but we are spending, so make sure that what we are going to buy we were going to buy anyway.

There are people who think that because they bought a state-of-the-art phone at $100 off they saved $100, but if it cost them $1,000, they actually spent $900 and that's what they weren't planning to do anyway.

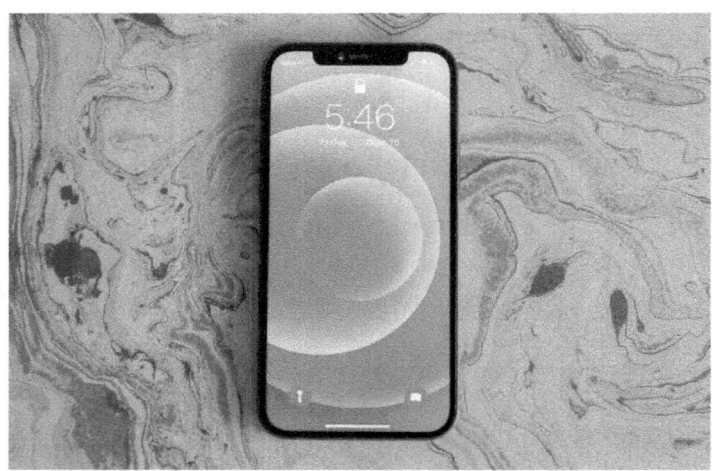

So, in this case it's about being conscious, about analyzing the possibilities, about not going into debt, because we practically eliminate and throw away all the benefits of saving. And in any case, be very, very intelligent with each decision I make, and write down each of these expenses so that we can see over time how our decision-making capacity evolves, the financial intelligence we have will be reflected in this expense application that shows us statistically how we have been with respect to income and expenses, and every month there should be a positive difference; income "x", expenses "y", and here is the difference with respect to savings.

This difference, remember, on a ratio basis but it should always be positive and not negative, if we count debt payments with monthly installments and so on. If you have debts and this makes it a little difficult for you to solve the savings issue, you should focus first on ending these or minimizing them and focus on saving.

In any case, it is a matter of getting into the habit right away with any amount of money, even if it seems to be very little.

Conclusion

Finally if none of this is enough, there is no other way, you need to earn more money, you need to focus on creating additional sources of income or increase your current source of income, you need to simply inject more capital into your financial life to manage it in the best way.

What happens is that there are many people who think that more money is going to be the solution, as I tell you there are people who earn 10 thousand dollars a month and it is not enough for them (some of them are in debt and the 10 thousand dollars is not enough to pay their debts and they spend years in debt spending ridiculous amounts of money in interest).

 So it is knowing that there is a trap there, in thinking that more money is going to solve the problem. So, really identify at what point I do need to earn more and start working as hard as possible to generate more and better income, but that I am at all times and at every stage of my life maximizing the return on everything that comes into my life financially.

So I hope you can apply these steps, it is a simple way to start and it is important that we apply each of the steps, as this will offer us better options in the future to spend our money on better things or other things of value.

Future

Undoubtedly, by being able to apply these methods that will allow you to not only to have a savings of your income, but to take the next leap to financial financial education and to be able to obtain what we want so much, such as a car or a house like a car or a house without having to leave a large percentage of our salary in interest interest, after you apply all these methods

I invite you to continue in the methods, I invite you to continue on the path of financial education, making better use of your money in the making a better use of your money in these last years by informing yourself or reading my next books where I deal with more advanced topics. advanced topics.